Persuade them

Public Speaking to Convince

John Zehring

Copyright 2019 John Zehring

TABLE OF CONTENTS

Introduction

Know Your Audience

Ten Key Rules for Public Speaking

Persuade Them

Capitalize on Your Language

Appear Capable and Trustworthy

Content

Delivery

About the Author

Public Speaking Books by John Zehring

Introduction

**"Not brute force
but only persuasion and faith
are the kings of this world."**
Thomas Carlyle

When I taught public speaking at a university, there were different types of speeches which students were assigned to deliver in class. There were informational speeches, special occasion speeches like introductions or presentations, and persuasive speeches. Students would be bumped up one grade if they could deliver a compelling persuasive speech about a topic which was opposite of their personal values or beliefs, without anyone detecting the ruse. The point was to learn the dynamics, techniques and style of speaking to persuade.

Your words and your delivery have incredible power to change someone, for good or for bad, to be used or misused. Persuasion is subtle, sometimes subconscious, and emotional. You could be persuaded to do something or think something that is not in your best interest by a master at persuasion. Persuasion is used to sell, to convince, to motivate and to change ideas, values or attitudes. You possess power. Your speaking to persuade has the power to inspire, challenge, change ideas or cause another to believe or act for a desired purpose.

Persuasive speeches can appeal to the mind or to the heart. When you use logic to attempt to persuade another, you present a set of information to show why listeners should accept the rational conclusion. When you appeal to the heart to persuade another, you attempt to make listeners feel a certain way so they will accept a conclusion.

Senator Everett Dirksen said *"The mind is no match with the heart in persuasion; constitutionality is no match with compassion."* Effective persuasive speakers appeal to both mind and heart.

You use persuasion at home and at work, in your social circles, and with organizations to which you belong. Persuasive skills can be a centerpiece of your career, making or breaking your advancement or success. Your ability to persuade another may be one of the most important skills you will ever use.

At its worst, persuasion is capable of shading the truth just a bit, doctoring quotes to fit the position, choosing selective statistics, passing off opinion as fact, pandering to prejudice or stereotypes, or playing on emotions. We have been on the receiving end of the misuse of persuasion, so we have a heightened interest in using persuasion with integrity and honor. Martin Luther King, Jr. said *"It is not possible to bring about a truly beneficial result by using unethical methods."* The ideal of effective persuasion is a good person speaking well. That is the intent of this book, to guide and encourage you to grow in skill as one who will employ your power for good.

There is a difference between your ability to talk to persuade and your skill in public speaking to persuade. In social settings, do we not admire people who can think quickly on their feet and make convincing arguments? That seems to be a natural gift. But speaking to persuade as a public speaker is a skill that can be learned and mastered. With proper research, preparation, editing, writing, practice and delivery, you can craft a presentation with power to change another's attitudes, values, beliefs or actions.

There are two parts to speeches: CONTENT and DELIVERY. Some prepare well, research, wrestle with the topic, connect the message to the audience, and deliver excellent information. For their content, they get an A+. The same speaker, on the other hand, may rate a C- on delivery. Perhaps the speaker does not make eye contact. Listeners do not feel seen. He does not even peek at you when he speaks, let alone linger in a gaze that causes you to feel like you and he are engaged in a conversation. She reads most of her speech. Perhaps ninety percent of the time his eyes are affixed upon the paper on the podium. She stares out the side window as though watching the traffic. If you could see behind the podium, he is making a few hand gestures, but they are mostly to himself, not to aid in the delivery. His and her messages are still valuable. Better to have great content with inadequate delivery than the other way around. Who would favor all sizzle and no steak? But why not master both content and delivery? This book aims to provide you with increased ability to connect with your audience to deliver a compelling persuasive public presentation.

You have used persuasive techniques since early childhood when you attempted to persuade your parents to give you what you wanted. Now, learn to hone your mastery of persuasive public speaking – avoiding known blunders and adopting proven strategies – to become proficient in speaking to persuade.

John Zehring

Some of this work is adapted from other books or eBooks I have written, which can be found at Amazon, Barnes and Noble, and other book sellers.

Know Your Audience

**"The best way to persuade people
is with your ears
– by listening to them."**
Dean Rusk

Knowing your audience and understanding their needs, feelings, views, objections, suspicions, questions, beliefs, openness to change their minds, and leanings is the #1 key to persuading others in public speaking. To persuade them, you must know them, understand them, and get into their shoes and walk a mile in them.

#2 is grasping that you are not addressing everyone in the audience but are pinpointing like a laser beam those whom you want to target where there is potential to persuade them to see things your way. You are not trying to persuade everyone. Some will never change their minds. Your efforts would be wasted on them. The ones whose hearts you reach out to touch are those who have the capability to hear your message, be influenced by your information, and adopt your position.

Beware of a big pitfall in attempting to persuade others, and that is starting with your own best arguments. For the moment, put down the many points you hope to score and instead, start with them. Look around you, sense the atmosphere, and pinpoint who in the audience you desire to reach. Unlike other types of public speaking, where you attempt to speak to everyone in the room, persuasive public speaking zeros-in on the handful of listeners who have the potential to be receptive to your arguments.

When you speak, there is one person in your audience who will significantly benefit from your presentation. You will never know who or how you motivated them. So, have confidence that you are making a difference. When you look deeply into the eyes of each listener, perhaps that is the one on that day who needs most what you have to offer.

The value of your preparation is multiplied exponentially when you connect with your listeners. Before you launch into your message, build rapport with your audience. Talk with them in a relaxed, informal manner. Bond with them. Like them and help them to like you. Relax and make small talk for a bit, as you might in a conversation. Do not rush to get down to business. The business will be wasted if you fail to connect.

Consider some strategies to evaluate and reach your audience:

HOW LISTENERS PROCESS PERSUASIVE MESSAGES: Persuasion is something a speaker does not TO an audience but WITH an audience. Listeners are all the while assessing the speaker's credibility, delivery, supporting materials, language, reasoning, emotional appeals, and non-verbal communication. Listeners are arguing inside their own minds with the speaker, engaging in a mental give and take. The more directly the topic bears on their lives, the more they engage in this internal conversation with the speaker. When you hit upon their *"hot buttons,"* they are engaged 100%. When you speak to persuade, remind yourself that listeners are holding a mental dialog with you.

NEVER PRESUME THEY AGREE WITH YOU. Have you ever been in the company of a person who presumed you agreed with them? They don't get it, do they? They assume too much. That dynamic alone can turn off those who are undecided or still working on which position they favor. Speaking to persuade yields better results if the speaker presumes nothing about positions held by the audience.

UNDERSTATE. A speaker who overstates a position, fact, or argument may turn off the very ones he or she hopes to convince. Understating has the opposite effect. Listeners assign higher credibility to a speaker who is careful with facts and who understates a position. The audience may be more easily persuaded to consider a position which is understated rather than the one which is biased or partisan. Exaggeration backfires. For example, if using a statistic, understate. Suppose that you are speaking about climate change and want to reveal that 86% of Americans believe that climate change is caused by human actions. Instead of saying that almost 90% believe that climate change is human-caused, understate by saying that more than 4 out of 5 Americans believe that climate change is human caused. The "almost" in the first appeal could be contested, whereas the understated "more than" in the second appeal uplifts your credibility.

SKEPTICAL LISTENERS CANNOT BE CONVERTED unless you deal directly with their reasons for skepticism. Identify and name reasons why people might not choose your position. That is exactly what is going on in their minds anyway: thinking of reasons why to reject your position. If you already name some of those reasons, you will be credited with being fair and understanding the other side of an issue. Then, you can proceed to emphasize why your position should be favored.

PROVIDE COUNTER-ARGUMENTS. Acknowledge that you know the other side's point of view. The more convincing you present the opposing positions, the bigger the bang when you provide an even stronger case for your own position. Great persuasive speeches begin with presenting counter-arguments so convincingly that listeners start to believe the speaker is actually arguing for them. Then, the speaker masterfully and politely explains why those arguments are insufficient. Present competing points of view fairly, and then refute them.

BE AS TOUGH ON YOUR SPEECH AS YOUR AUDIENCE WILL BE. Test it out in advance with a friend or family member who will provide a constructive critique of your arguments, data, and appeal. Passion and enthusiasm for a position can be fraught with blind spots. Better to have a friend reveal your blind spots in advance than the ones you hope to persuade.

IF YOU SLIGHT THE OTHER SIDE, you lose. Never attack another speaker. Attack arguments, not individuals. Even if listeners agree with your position, they will mentally dismiss you if you slight another.

YOU DO NOT HAVE TO WIN EVERY BATTLE. The goal is to win the war, not every battle. The goal is to persuade for a position overall. Do not require listeners to agree with 100% of every case that you make. Ask them to agree with your general position while acknowledging that they might still be working on some of the pieces and parts.

YOU DO NOT HAVE TO PERSUADE EVERY LISTENER. Baseball players do not bat 1,000 and neither will persuasive speakers. Be kind and gentle to those who will not agree, but do not consider yourself a failure if you do not convince everyone. Therefore, narrow in like a laser beam on your target audience: who specifically do you want to reach most?

SHOW A NEED. Convince listeners there is a problem. The burden of proof is on the speaker to convince listeners that the old way is not working. Then, present a plan for solving the need. Demonstrate why and how it will work. Show how a similar plan was successfully implemented elsewhere. Or, if your position is to oppose a change or a shift, argue that change is impractical and that it will create more problems than it will solve.

VISUALIZE. Help your listeners to visualize benefits to them. Draw word pictures of what their lives might look like if they concur with the position you present. Use vivid imagery to show listeners how they will gain.

MAKE YOUR LISTENERS FEEL IMPORTANT. Mary Kay Ash said *"Pretend that every single person you meet has a sign around his or her neck that says, 'Make me feel important.' Not only will you succeed in sales, you will succeed in life."* Show respect for your listeners. If each one feels that you believe they are important, openness to your arguments will skyrocket.

ACTION: Define what you want the audience to do. Explain how. Conclude with a stirring appeal that reinforces their commitment to act.

How to size-up your audience

Conduct an off-the-cuff audience analysis. Observe the audience to note about what you analyze about their situation. Consider the group's composition by age, gender, socio-economic status, cultural diversity, racial and ethnic background, sexual orientation, religion, group membership, political leanings, occupations represented, educational level, and interests such as sports, arts, travel, music, and so on. Then consider how those factors might influence your choice of language. For example, in a group where 95% have zero interest in classical music, illustrations about Toscanini or Heifetz might bore. On the other hand, speaking to managers about how to help difficult employees get along with one another might strike a chord that appeals to most of them. When you first see your audience, ask yourself: what are my assumptions about this group of people?

SIZE: Speakers can find a small audience more difficult than a large audience. A more formal speech that works with a crowd may fail with a dozen or two listeners. A chatty informal folksy talk that works well with a small audience may fall flat with a large audience expecting a well-edited, thought-provoking presentation. Adapt your delivery to fit the size. If you are behind a podium addressing hundreds of listeners, your delivery will be different than if you are seated around a table with half a dozen colleagues. In the larger case, employ public speaking techniques. In the smaller case, prepare and practice well, but here you are more "talking with" than "delivering" your presentation. Picture yourself in the audience and ask how you would respond to the delivery style you intend. Are you an invited guest speaking to strangers or are you a familiar member speaking to people with whom you work, live, or volunteer with every day? Adjust your delivery to your audience.

PHYSICAL SETTING: What will be your plan if there are distractions, such as a baby crying or a cell phone ringing? If an obnoxious ringtone goes off, will you ignore it or acknowledge it? Sometimes it serves you well to acknowledge it kindly: "That happens to all of us once in a while." If you demonstrate a non-anxious presence with distractions, your listeners will relax and stay with you.

AGE: Focus on the audience's interests more than your own. Tailor illustrations to their age, not yours. If they are mostly the Medicare set and you are still carving out your career, speak less about relationships with bosses or co-workers -- your audience is not employed. If your audience is composed significantly of college-age people, illustrations about internships, networking, appearance, and careers will have more appeal than tips on how to apply for Medicare. People like to feel like they are learning about something that relates to them.

ASK: You can learn about your audience by simply asking them… "How many of you…?" When I taught a class of university students, most in their early twenties, I asked them:
How many of you prefer CATS to DOGS? Prefer DOGS?
How many of you like SPORTS? Are not interested…?
How many of you are MARRIED? Have CHILDREN?
For how many of you was this SCHOOL your 1st choice?
How many of you currently WORK fifteen hours a week or more?
How many of you are NATIVES to this state?
How many of you VOLUNTEER on a regular basis?
How many of you love JAZZ? CLASSICAL? COUNTRY? RAPP? ROCK?
How many of you intend to become a MILLIONAIRE in your lifetime?
How many of you are IN LOVE?

How many of you EXERCISE at least three times a week? How many of you are under some STRESS right now?

Some of the questions were light, as a way to warm them up to more serious inquiries. After this ninety-second survey, I was able to add more data to my audience analysis: millionaire rated high. Love less so. Most worked part-time or more. More than half volunteered. All were experiencing some stress.

I was speaking at a retirement complex where I had spoken before, but this time, the listeners did not seem to be with me. They smiled politely, yet appeared to be preoccupied and even distracted. Something was not right, but I did not know what it was. Afterward I learned that one of their beloved members had died the evening before. They were grieving, mourning, and looking for comfort and assurance.

What should I have done? Answer: Always work the crowds for a few minutes before your presentation. Forget the grand entrance. Walk around, greet them, and ask them how they are or is everybody okay today? This is the time to do a lot of listening, not talking. Touch them, shake hands, pat a shoulder, or if appropriate, give a hug. Make yourself highly accessible beforehand. Had I done that, I would have gathered information that would have helped me to shift the presentation to meet their needs that day.

Great public speakers are AUDIENCE-CENTERED. As I prepare for presentations, I have found it useful to close my eyes and repeat: "It's not about me. It's not about me. It's not about me. It's about them and their interests. Not my interests."

HONOR YOUR AUDIENCE. A simple exercise is to calculate how many "people minutes" are used in your speech. For example, if there are two hundred listeners and your speech is twelve minutes long, that is 2,400 minutes of cumulative time, or forty hours. That tells me that my brief presentation is worth forty hours of my audience's time. I do not want to waste their time. I want to do my best for them. They hold high expectations of what they desire to receive, which calls for high preparation and effort in content and delivery.

As a public speaker, you have power to persuade. Use your power to effect change for that which is good. Recognize you have power when you speak. Use your power responsibly.

Ten Key Rules for Public Speaking

"Don't raise your voice, improve your argument."
Desmond Tutu

My wife's grandfather earned his living as an architectural renditionist. Before computers, he would draw a rendition of what the architect's plans would look like when completed. By avocation, he was an artist who drew scenes of Philadelphia's Independence Hall, Williamsburg's Governor's Palace, and of Maine's Friendship Harbor. I asked him if he ever delved into modern art. He told me that he was not yet good enough to paint modern art, because an artist must first master the rules before breaking them. Picasso, he added, was first taught by his father, Professor Ruiz, who believed that proper training required disciplined copying of the masters. Picasso was capable of forging the Old Masters before he broke the rules to depict a new way of seeing. So too with public speaking: first master the rules. Break them not until you know what you are doing and why. Now, the rules:

One: Write for the ear.

A danger is that what you write may end up like something to be read rather than to be heard. When you prepare for a speech, what do you do? You go to your keyboard and compose. You write it out. But that is writing, usually to be read. Consider the difference between writing a story for a newspaper and writing the same for the radio. It is a different style of writing. People read the newspaper but listen to the radio. Likewise, people listen to your speech. So, a speech must be written for the ear, not the eye.

When writing a message, talk it out loud as you write to see how it sounds to you. Imagine how it will be heard by your listeners. Rehearse it out loud before delivering it. Commandment number one: write for the ear, not for the eye.

Two: Make every word tell.

This comes from one of the greatest style manuals ever written. In *The Elements of Style* by William Strunk, Jr. and E. B. White, one of the utmost pieces of advice to writers ever given is this:

Vigorous writing is concise. A sentence should contain no unnecessary words, a paragraph no unnecessary sentences, for the same reason that a drawing should have no unnecessary lines and a machine no unnecessary parts. This requires not that the writer make all his sentences short, or that he avoid all detail and treat his subjects only in outline, but that every word tell.

Strunk and White's counsel is to omit needless words. All writing should be clear, plain, active and concise. When writing for the ear, clear and concise writing is cherished by listeners.

In a speech, it is the power of language that grabs listeners. Think of great speeches you have heard and how the speakers moved people by their words. What counted most? It was not necessarily eye contact, important as that is: Winston Churchill did not make eye contact. It was not that the speaker looked too much at notes: Nelson Mandela hardly looked up from his written manuscript.

It was not the length of the speech: Ronald Regan's eulogy to the Challenger astronauts captured in fifty-one seconds what it might take many of us fifteen minutes to say and we could never say it so eloquently.

Winston Churchill said *"Short words are best and the old words when short are best of all."* Plato, Lincoln, Jesus, and Martin Luther King, Jr. employed mostly words of one or two syllables. Lincoln's Gettysburg Address contains 271 words and all but twenty are only one or two syllables. Favor short words, short sentences, and active verbs. Consider some classic lines:
These are the times that try men's souls
It was the best of times, it was the worst of times.
Two roads diverged into a yellow wood... and I took the one less traveled by.
Ask not what your country can do for you...
I have a dream...
The Lord is my shepherd, I shall not want.
To be, or not to be, that is the question.

Do you notice the obvious? Most are short words of one or two syllables. When you invest your effort to craft the message and weave the words together, your audience will be grateful, will remember, and will be moved because listeners appreciate outstanding communication. Make every word tell.

Three: Use *"you"* words.

The first person singular is the pronoun cherished by listeners: *I, me* or *mine*. We like those and use them most. Are not most listeners drawn in by the word *"me"*? From the podium, the word *"you"* has the same effect: it is well received and causes the listener to pay careful attention because *"the speaker is talking to me."* When you use the word *"you"* in public speaking, use it in the singular, not the plural. That is, speak to *"you"* as an individual, not to *you* as a group of people... *"you people."* Speaking to *"you all"* loses the impact of speaking to one person... to me. Consider:
"I am glad you are here today" makes it sound like you are glad I am present.
"I am glad you are all here today" makes me just one of a bunch, noticed or not.

Unlearn the use of the word *"one"* when referring to a person. That might have been a favored style for college papers, but in speaking, it sounds awful: One goes, one does, one reads, one speaks. *"When one is considering the alternatives"* sounds like it refers to someone else. *"When you are considering the alternatives"* sounds like the speaker is addressing me. Remember: as a listener, I like the word *"me"*.

There is little danger in overuse of the word *"you"* in your presentations. Using *"you"* words sounds more conversational and entices the hearer to listen with heightened attention. The greater danger is to underuse *"you"* words, which could end up sounding like your speech is more like a paper prepared for a college or graduate school course.

When I taught university students, most of whom were in their early twenties, I allowed them three uses maximum of the hackneyed term *"you guys."* After the maximum was reached, their grade was reduced a notch each time they said *"you guys."* When I dine out, the waitress or waiter frequently greets us with *"How are you guys tonight?"* That is fine for waiters or waitresses and used once or twice it sounds personal. In a speech, it would be better to avoid the term *"guys"* as though you are trying to be a buddy to your audience. On the other hand, pepper your messages well with *"you"* words.

Four: Any method of delivery is okay except for reading your manuscript.

Which is the most effective method of delivery? Here are three keys: 1) it's not the method. 2) it's not the method. 3) it's not the method. There is no magical method, no secret formula, and no one single correct way. Some presentations are charismatic, funny, entertaining, enlightening, motivational, inspiring, or moving. Others are matter of fact, informative, educational, instructive or enlightening. The best method of delivery is what works best for you and suits you.

You are well-served to experiment and find the method that fits you best. Except one: reading. Do not read a speech. Reading a work meant to be spoken is the deadliest of all methods. There is nothing wrong with practicing your message so many times that you do not really need it except as a point of reference. Then, you will not be dependent upon your manuscript and can focus upon the delivery to an audience waiting to be led by you.

A classic study in educational psychology set up an experiment to determine how much an audience PERCEIVES it is learning. In the audience were a few hundred graduate level students. The speaker for the control group was an actual scholar who gave a lecture, primarily reading from notes. His content revealed some actual groundbreaking content. The speaker for the experimental group was an actor decked out with phony credentials from non-existent schools, phony publications from journals which were a figment of the imagination, and a message filled with contradictions, false information, excessive use of double talk, jargon, neologisms, phony statistics, and inaccurate data. However, the actor was winsome, humorous, and appeared to speak extemporaneously without notes. He exuded charisma, oozed an attractive personality, and possessed a twinkle in his eye and a gleam in his smile. Afterward, the listeners were invited to rate each lecture. Overwhelmingly, the audience felt it had learned more from the entertaining actor. This became know as the "Dr. Fox Effect," named after the lecturer decked out with phony credentials. The actor had fooled the entire audience of graduate students into thinking they had learned more and they enjoyed it too. None discovered the ruse. The outcome of this experiment is not to encourage public speakers to dazzle with mere charisma, but the effects were clear: speakers who use humor, who are not tethered to notes, and who connect well with their audience will be perceived as the most effective and even the most credible.

The study also made clear: those who read from the podium or podium will be perceived as less effective… or ineffective. Whether you use a manuscript, cards, an outline or memory, use what suits you best. Any method is acceptable, except reading from notes.

Five: Eye contact is greater than the points you want to make.

Make eye contact with your listeners. Glancing up from your manuscript for a millisecond to stare into middle distance does not count as eye contact. Looking at no one in particular is not eye contact. Even a fleeting peek at an individual hardly rates. When you are in an audience, don't you enjoy it when the speaker looks at you, sees you, and then you feel like you are connecting personally?

Remind yourself to linger. Linger awhile on one person's eyes and then move to another and tarry for a while, looking at them while you speak. Even if you linger on a listener only once or twice, they will feel seen. Noticed. Connected. How long is a lingering gaze? It is more than a second or two. Practice lingering eye contact the next time you speak. Lingering too long can make the other feel uncomfortable, as though you are drilling down on them. Five or six seconds seems a good length. Then, your listeners will perceive that you are speaking to them personally, they will believe they are learning more, and they will form a bond with you as a person, rather than as a talking head who talks AT his or her listeners.

Draw reminder graphics to yourself on your manuscript or outline to signal where eye contact is most needed. When I felt it was especially important to be looking at the audience rather than at notes, I drew a pair of eyes in the margin of my notes.

Another margin note I find helpful is to draw a pair of eyes with the mathematical *greater than* symbol followed by a few dots, representing the points I want to make: *oo* > ... That reminded me that eye contact is greater than the exact points I intended to make.

That was difficult for me, because I try to write in an organized way and want to make my points clear. The reality is, they are not going to remember all my points, but they will remember that they felt seen. That evolves into the perception, accurate or not, that they learned something or gained a new perspective. Eye contact is greater than making all the points.

Six: Prepare one hour for each minute of the message.

That's the norm. Perhaps it is not as daunting as it sounds. Preparation includes struggling for the right idea and approach to the message; reading, study and research; outlining, drafting, rewriting and editing; practicing out loud; and delivery. It is possible you will invest even more than an hour for each minute of the speech, especially when your audience expects the highest quality from you.

Speaking uses every ounce of creative energy you possess, and then some. It is also a most satisfying opportunity. Crafting a creative work to help your listeners grow, learn, be motivated or persuaded is a satisfying way to invest yourself.

An experienced musician might play extemporaneously, to the entertainment of listeners. Most often, musicians practice and rehearse for hours – much like public speakers. To improve at any skill or art, practice, practice, practice.

Rehearse your message out loud, four or five times if possible. Stand in front of a mirror, use an audio or video recorder, or just practice it, but nothing prepares you better for the actual presentation than practicing out loud. Most important, practice out loud *on your feet*. Mimic as closely as possible the feel of the real experience of delivery.

Practice the same time of day (e.g., morning, afternoon or evening) that you will deliver your presentation so that you capture the mood of the time of day. Pay attention to your non-verbal communication and to your use of pause, timing, and gestures. After you have practiced well, editing and cleaning up as you go, you will feel ready.

An advantage of the rule of one hour in the study for each minute behind the podium is that it forces you to keep your messages briefer. Perhaps you have heard the old adage about speeches: *If you haven't struck oil after twenty minutes, stop boring.* A twenty-minute speech is long for the audience to stay with you. Many of the greatest messages are ten to fifteen minutes long. A fifteen-minute message is hard to accomplish. It is far easier to write a long message. To create an excellent fifteen-minute work requires substantial rewriting and editing, which is to your advantage as well as to your audience's delight. Few listeners have asked for a longer speech and they most certainly appreciate a tightly edited and well-crafted work.

When you have rehearsed out loud a number of times, you hit a point when you know you are ready. In fact, you are eager. You cannot wait to reach the podium and begin. The excitement in your voice becomes contagious as listeners can sense you know where you are going and what you want to accomplish. Enthusiasm is a winning tool for the art of persuasion.

If you are able to prepare your presentation at least a week or more in advance, you have the advantage of being able to rehearse once a day prior to your delivery. There is no last-minute panic, rush or worry about how it will come together.

There is a strange phenomenon experienced by public speakers. When you stand up and look into the eyes of your listeners, there can be a feeling of *"I just want to get this over with."* That could lead to rushing, which undoes all the good work and preparation you invested. Practicing a few times out loud and on your feet prepares you to relax, to avoid that *"get it over with"* feeling, and to enjoy making your presentation.

Baseball great Yogi Berra said *"People don't want to hear about the labor, they want to see the baby."* Avoid the temptation to bore listeners with how hard you worked to research, prepare, write or wrestle with the topic. It's not about you. It's about them. Lift THEM up and embrace them, and you will have them listening to you on the edge of their seats.

Of all the suggestions or commandments about public speaking, perhaps this one should be first: Practice, practice, practice – out loud and on your feet. Total effort: one-hour prep for each minute of delivery.

Seven: Edit the hell out of it.

First drafts are rarely that good and you are probably not the best editor of your work. It would be wonderful if you could get another to edit your work, but that is unlikely. And so, consider your first draft as just that: a draft. Research, outline, get it down on paper, and then edit. Some of the greatest writers edit their works dozens of times. Author James Michener once said *"I am not that good a writer, but I am one hell of a rewriter."* Oh that a speaker would care so much for the outcome that he or she would edit and rewrite.

Pianist Artur Schnabel said *"The notes I handle no better than many pianists. But the pauses between the notes -- ah, that is where the art resides."* With speaking, the art resides in the editing and rewriting.

Eight: A good message has a good beginning, a good ending, and both close together.

Invest the most time on your introduction and conclusion. Have you ever noticed that people talk longer when they know the least… or are the least prepared… or are disorganized? If you grab your audience at the beginning, they will follow you into the rest of the message. A good beginning, like a picture, is worth a thousand words. Imagine hearing *"I'd like to tell you a story…"* Your audience will lean forward with interest to hear a story. Follow the model of journalism: Many news stories begin with a concrete example or illustration. They tell a story about an individual and then fan out with the broader story. Start with a specific before applying general principles.

Your conclusion should leave listeners wanting more, thinking, motivated, considering, inspired, persuaded, or at least glad they came to hear you speak. If appropriate, tie your ending to the beginning. When preparing a speech, finding the ending can be a challenge. When in doubt, always go up. Frequently, the best conclusion already exists a few paragraphs up.

"…and both close together." Do not mistake quantity for quality. A well-educated audience will recognize good organization and will appreciate fine editing. If you labor to shorten rather than to lengthen your message, it will show. Strive to bring your beginning and your ending closer together. A good message is always shorter than your audience's attention span.

Nine: Manage nervousness and use it creatively.

American's top fear is not the fear of heights, water, snakes, darkness, or getting peanut butter stuck to the roof of the mouth. The #1 fear is the fear of public speaking. Emerson said *"Fear defeats more people than any other one thing in the world."*

The #1 antidote is to manage fear and to use it in your favor. Your listeners are glad they are not the one up there speaking publicly. When you come across with humility, they will cut you some slack and forgive your mistakes.

Know that even though you feel nervous, the audience does not know you are nervous unless you tell them. The biggest mistake you can make is to draw attention to a mistake or to your nervousness. Chances are high listeners will not remember a mistake even if they notice it. They are listening for your content and are not paying attention to your nervous stomach or shaking knees. Do not let it show. Do not draw attention to it.

Everyone gets nervous when they speak before a group. If you are not nervous, you could be in trouble! Speakers who claim to be *cool as a cucumber* are generally as thick-skinned as a cucumber and about as inspiring as a cucumber. The key is not to rid yourself of nervousness but to learn to manage nervousness for your advantage.

To be nervous means you care to do your best. Your nervousness will keep every nerve of your body focused on your listeners and on your delivery. Nervousness is nature's way of preparing you to meet the challenge.

Nervousness keeps you on your toes, alert to your audience, thinking faster, talking more fluidly, and speaking with greater intensity and enthusiasm. If nervousness shows in your voice or body, it is not a drawback. Your audience will have sympathy with you and appreciation for your effort in the face of discomfort. Remember, your audience will not be paying attention to your nervousness or to mistakes… unless you tell them.

Preparation and practice (out loud and on your feet) can reduce stage fright by up to 75%. Practice gives you the sense that *"I know it, I like it, and I'm ready."* Practice helps you to maintain control, which feels good, and to even learn to enjoy speaking before a group rather than to wish to get it over with as soon as possible.

A well-known speaker was asked if she enjoyed speaking. She answered *"Before my speech, I am an anxious mess. During the speech, I am in agony. After the speech, I am completely exhausted. But to answer your question, yes. I love to speak publicly."*

The #1 fear is not conquered by eliminating it, but by managing it and gaining control.

Ten: Use the "as if" principle.

This comes from Norman Vincent Peale, perhaps best known for his book *The Power of Positive Thinking*. Lesser known was the fact that Peale taught public speaking at a night school and that is where he developed the *as if* principle: "Act *as if*, and that which you practice will tend to be. If, for example, you are fearful but want to have courage, act *as if* you did have courage and in time you will have courage.

Similarly, if you are lacking in enthusiasm, act *as if* you were enthusiastic and your personality will begin to be just that."

Peale tells of an incident when he taught a class in public speaking. One student was completely desultory and uninspired in his platform presentation. *"You need enthusiasm,"* Peale said.

"I know," the man replied, *"but you cannot be enthusiastic just by wanting it."*

"Oh, yes you can," Peale insisted. *"Next time you speak, act really enthusiastic. Pour it on, give it all you've got."*

"That will be phony. You can't be enthusiastic just by acting as if you were," the student remonstrated.

Peale continued to encourage him to employ the *as if* principle. "The next time he was the speaker, he really threw himself into his talk and the reaction of his hearers was electric. So inspired was this hitherto dull speaker that he continued to act *as if* he were the most enthusiastic of all speakers until in due course he honestly qualified for that category. To have enthusiasm, act *as if* you possess it and you shall have it."

In your speaking, act like you have enthusiasm for your topic and your audience will capture it. Act like you have courage in public speaking, and you will grow into it. Act confident and you will truly become self-confident.

Persuade Them

**"People almost invariably arrive at their beliefs
not on the basis of proof but
on the basis of what they find attractive."**
Blaise Pascal

GET THEM WITH YOU. Rather than rushing in to quickly score points, invest time well by building rapport. Talk with them. Smile. Start on the upbeat. Help them to feel that they are having a conversation with you. Interact: ask them a few questions. Build a positive atmosphere by asking questions to which they will answer *yes*. Get them in a yes mood. Build trust. Help them to like you and have confidence in your grasp on the topic. The time you spend at the beginning to get the audience with you may be the most important part of your presentation. Abraham Lincoln advised *"If you wish to win a man over to your ideas, first make him your friend."* Befriend your listeners.

EMPHASIZE WHAT THEY WILL GAIN. Appeal to their self-interest. How will they personally benefit from adopting your position? Don't overwhelm. Zero in on two or three ways they will reap some benefit. Will they gain economically? How could your position benefit their quality of life, their health, their career advancement, or their enjoyment? Appeal also to their altruistic instincts. If appropriate, tell how your position will benefit the company, organization, church, neighborhood, community or world. All the while you are speaking, they are wondering how your position might affect them personally. Answer up front how they will gain. If you cannot do that, how then do you expect them to answer it for themselves?

TALK ABOUT WHAT THEY WILL LOSE. What is the downside for them if they do not accept your position? Will they lose money? Will their quality of life diminish? Could their career or standing in the community be jeopardized? Take care not to over-do it. If you make it sound like the sky is falling, they might write you off or decide the case is hopeless. Overstate, and you lose. Dwight Eisenhower said *"I would rather try to persuade a man to go along, because once I have persuaded him, he will stick. If I scare him, he will stay just as long as he is scared, and then he is gone."* Use facts. Use examples. If possible, tell how others have lost by not adopting your stance. People tend to be more persuadable when they are confronted with loss, rather than gain. People are inclined to be lose averse. Tell them your proposal might help the organization gain $50,000 and they might be interested, but warning them that the organization might lose $50,000 if your proposal is not accepted and they are more likely to jump on board your position. This is because people tend to become attached to what they already have and fear losing it.

GUIDE THEM TO THINK THROUGH THE IDEA. Consider how people learn. Learning by discovery is the most powerful. Learning by being lectured to pales in comparison. Guide their thinking. If possible, let them to think that they came up with the idea. Blaise Pascal wrote *"People are generally better persuaded by the reasons which they have themselves discovered than by those which have come into the mind of others."* Nelson Mandela put it this way: *"It is wise to persuade people to do things and make them think it was their own idea."* Suppose, for example, you are attempting to convince your organization to put on a new roof. After you have built rapport, established trust, and conversed back and forth, and after you have pointed out what they will gain and what they will lose, create a sense of urgency.

The roof is leaking, damage could be occurring behind the walls, the ceilings are becoming ruined, and mold may be forming which could risk health problems. On the other hand, funds are scarce. Perhaps we should wait to see how bad the damage could become, although that might cost more in the long run. Help them to weigh the pros and cons and believe that they have only one choice.

TUG AT THEIR NEED FOR CONSISTANCY. People feel the need to remain consistent with their past actions. Suppose, for example, you are making the case for your business to increase charitable giving to local community organizations. Giving is not only being a good neighbor and building trust within the community, but it helps your business's name recognition. Which increases sales. But business is tight right now and something must be cut. Emphasize how you have been a community giver for long time. It is consistent with the business's past actions to continue. If your listeners have examples in their memory of that, they will want to continue to be consistent with their history.

CREATE A SENSE THAT EVERYONE ELSE IS DOING IT. Children use this argument when attempting to convince their parents that they should be allowed to do something. Everyone's going to the party. Everyone's allowed to drive with friends. Everyone's buying the red one. A famous study was conducted by Solomon Asch, known as The Asch Experiment, which demonstrated how peer pressure influences an opinion to conform. If, for example, you are attempting to persuade your organization to employ a consultant to make your website come alive and grab the attention of others, point out how everyone else is doing it. Give one or two concrete examples of competing organizations which have done it, including organizations that they know, admire, or respect.

What listeners hear: If one or two competitors are doing it, there must be a ton of people already doing it, so we better do it or we'll be left in the dust.

AIM HIGH. THEN, SHOW YOU ARE WILLING TO COMPROMISE. Set a high bar. Suppose you are making the case that your community organization should ask donors to increase their giving by ten percent. Members of the Board of Directors balk, realizing that they are among top donors already. A couple suggest no increase. But that is not realistic, for cost of living increases are needed to avoid cuts in program. So, you demonstrate a willingness to hear their views and compromise. Together you come up with a more realistic request to ask for a five percent increase.

MAKE A STRONG COUNTERARGUMENT TO YOUR POSITION. This feels like turning your car on ice into the direction of the skid, aiming directly at the telephone pole. It feels counterintuitive. However, if you show that you know well the points of the opposing position and you present them fairly, you are then open to shooting them down point by point. Your presentation is always strong and persuasive if you embrace the opposing side, weigh the pros and cons, and end up with your position being the best choice. If you can make compelling points for the opposite of your position, listeners will also assign you increased credibility, trust and appreciation.

EMPLOY HUMOR. Show that you do not take yourself too seriously. Get them laughing. If you are good at using humor, this is a key to lighten things up and win an audience's confidence. If you are not good at using humor, don't even try. Your best attempts will be destroyed if you flub. At the least, smile and get them smiling. Try to lighten up your position, especially at the beginning, and get people to laugh or lighten up.

They will be happier, they will associate you with happiness, and they will be that much more easily persuaded.

PEOPLE LOVE TO LISTEN TO THAT WHICH THEY ARE INTERESTED IN. That is why it is so important to know your audience and understand their interests. If you focus upon a topic which embraces their heightened interest, you grab their attention into the palm of your hand and they will like you all the more for connecting with them.

PERSISTANCE PAYS. People appreciate your enthusiasm, your positive energy, and your commitment. Keep hammering away at your desired outcome. If they seem inclined to dismiss your arguments, keep up your persistence and passion. A few will be persuaded by your persistence alone. Remember, every strategy you employ does not need to reach everybody. If each tip wins over a couple, soon you will have a critical mass agreeing with your position.

EXUDE CONFIDENCE. Humans respect a person who feels confident about his or her position. The more you act like you know what you are talking about and are deeply committed to your position, the higher listeners assign you credibility. And, the more credible you appear, the more trustworthy you are.

CONTROL HOW FAST YOU SPEAK. If your listeners seem not to agree, speak quickly. Speak slowly if they do. If they do not agree, speaking quickly does not give them time to formulate counterarguments. If they do agree, speak slowly so they can take in every word and become more persuaded.

LOOK AND SOUND ENTHUSIASTIC. Your enthusiasm for a position is a winning tool. Control your nervousness and use it to your advantage. Let your posture and your non-verbal communication exude enthusiasm. Your physical demeanor telegraphs a message to affirm or deny your commitment to your position.

GIVE THEM SOMETHING. Recipients respond with heightened affirmation if you give them something. For example, a chain of Italian restaurants offered diners a free glass of red wine with their dinner. It was unexpected. Free. A gift. Tips increased dramatically. The point is that people feel obliged to give something back in reciprocity for a gift that they have received. If a colleague does you a favor, then it feels like you owe that colleague a favor. In a study of restaurant tipping, the question was raised: Does the giving of a mint have any influence over how much tip you will leave them? Most people will say no. But that mint can make a surprising difference. In the study, giving diners a single mint at the end of their meal typically increased tips by around 3%. Interestingly, if the gift is doubled and two mints are provided, tips don't double. They quadruple – a 14% increase in tips. Perhaps most interesting of all is the fact that if the waiter provides one mint, starts to walk away from the table, but pauses, turns back and says, "For you nice people, here's an extra mint," tips go through the roof. A 23% increase, influenced not by what was given, but how it was given. So, if you can be the first to give something and to ensure that what you give is personalized and unexpected, it increases your chances of a positive response. This is not always possible in public speaking, but a plate of chocolate chip cookies or a bowl of tasty candies offered to your audience "in appreciation for their attention" to your presentation can have positive benefits. Remember, never is your goal to win over everyone. You win them one by one.

ESTABLISH YOUR EXPERTISE. People follow the lead of credible, knowledgeable experts. Physiotherapists, for example, are able to persuade more of their patients to comply with recommended exercise programs if they display their medical diplomas on the walls of their consulting rooms. It is important to signal to others what makes you a credible, knowledgeable authority before you make your influence attempt. When possible, arrange for another to introduce you who is not only connected to you but who is also likely to increase your credibility before your audience. It helps if they emphasize your years of experience, degrees, credentials, publications, or particular expertise in the subject.

GET THEM TO LIKE YOU. People prefer to say *yes* to those whom they like. We like people who are similar to us, we like people who pay us compliments, and we like people who cooperate with us towards mutual goals. So, instead of quickly getting down to business, interact with your audience to get to know them and for them to know about you. Share not only professional but personal information about yourself. If people know that you have children, like to ski or boat, or have some health disorder, they relate to you as a fellow human being... which means they like you more, trust you more, and are more receptive to your position.

Capitalize on Your Language

"The tongue can paint what the eye cannot see."
Chinese Proverb

USE LANGUAGE ACCURATELY. Misuse of grammar, verb tense, slang, *"um's"* and *"you know"* and *"yous guys"* will cause an audience to disregard your ability to say much to them. Mark Twain nailed it when he wrote *"The difference between the right word and the almost right word is the difference between lightning and the lightning bug."*

CHOOSE FAMILIAR WORDS. Build rapport with your audience. You do not want your audience to consider you long-winded, stuffy, ostentatious, self-righteous, or a show-off.

FAVOR CONCRETE WORDS rather than the abstract. Choose the specific rather than the general. Give a single, specific illustration or story and then, if needed, fan out from there to generalized applications.

EDIT TO ELIMINATE CLUTTER. Make your writing as tight as possible. Omit needless words.

ELIMINATE EXCESSIVE USE OF PHRASES or superlatives like *"very."* Let your verbs do the heavy lifting. Active verbs power a sentence. Decrease overuse of the verb *"to be."* While it is acceptable to use *"is,"* *"was,"* or *"am,"* edit to replace them with action verbs wherever possible.

APPEAL TO THEIR SENSES. Make them smell the bacon cooking over the campfire. Craft word pictures to appeal to seeing, hearing, tasting, smelling and touching.

EMPLOY METAPHOR. A metaphor is a comparison, sometimes subtle, but does not use the word *"like"* or *"as."* With metaphor, one thing stands for another to illustrate a greater truth or mystery.

EXPERIMENT WITH RHYTHM. *"I have a dream,"* spoke Martin Luther King, Jr., as he mastered a cadence that musically delivered one of the greatest speeches ever given. Learn from him: couple rhythm with repetition to drive home the point which will be remembered. When Senator Margaret Chase Smith's name was placed in nomination for the presidency of the United States, she stood at the microphone and said *"I speak as a Republican. I speak as a woman. I speak as a United States Senator. I speak as an American."* A little use of rhythm and repetition goes a long way. Too much can be considered gimmicky.

FAVOR SHORT SENTENCES. Use more periods and fewer commas. Long run-on sentences lose your audience's attention. Not all sentences must be short, but most should be. While shorter sentences and fewer complex words applies to the written word, it is needed even more when writing for the ear.

REDUCE POLYSYLLABIC WORDS. Choose the simpler word. Most Americans read on an eighth or ninth-grade reading level. The more words with three or more syllables you use, the higher the reading level required. Use too many polysyllabic words and your speech may be on the grade twenty-five reading level – far too high for most listeners to grasp. Then, they stop listening.

Appear Capable and Trustworthy

**"To be persuasive we must be believable;
to be believable we must be credible;
to be credible we must be truthful."**
Edward R. Murrow

Your credibility rests in the perception of the audience. How do they perceive you? Are they accurate? Perhaps, or maybe not. A speaker's credibility can be affected by the speaker's charisma, charm, sparkle, humor, smile, sociability, physical attractiveness, or connectivity with the audience. A highly credible speaker may not be perceived that way, whereas a phony can win them over and fool them into thinking the speaker is trustworthy. Why do listeners accept one speaker's view and reject those of another? The audience might be won over by the speaker's evidence, convinced by the speaker's reasoning, or their emotions touched by the speaker's ideas, language, stories, humor, sincerity, style or delivery.

Some days it does not seem fair. One observer suggested that *"Leadership is 95% personality."* Perhaps that is hyperbole, but there is some truth to it. And so, employ the best tools in your speaker's toolbox to build your credibility.

GOOD ORGANIZATION is perceived as containing higher credibility.

LANGUAGE which is appropriate, clear, and vivid strikes the audience as trustworthy. When an audience understands the message, they like the speaker.

DELIVERY counts. Prepare and practice, practice, practice. An old parody on speaking stated: *"Make them laugh, make them cry, make them feel motivated."*

SHOW CONCERN for the well-being of the audience. Establish common ground with the audience... what you have in common with them. Refer to their place, feelings, needs or interests. Listeners resonate to speakers who connect to their interests. These are the ones who say *"I felt she was speaking directly to me."*

GIVE EVIDENCE. The Scottish philosopher David Hulme noted that *"A wise person proportions his or her belief to the evidence."* The perception of a speaker's evidence is what sways an audience to assign credibility and trustworthiness. Cite sources. *"According to the internet..."* fails to show credibility.

EXPLAIN YOUR COMPETENCE. Not boastfully, but tell about why your reasoning is credible. Explaining your preparation and research rates higher than resting on credentials.

GET THEM NODDING THEIR HEADS rather than shaking their heads. If you asked three questions and each solicited a negative answer, you put the listener in a negative frame of mind. Flip the coin: ask three questions that draw affirmation and that creates a positive mood. Never underestimate the mood of a listener.

SPEAK WITH GENUINE CONVICTION. Believe what you say. If you demonstrate enthusiasm or excitement, listeners will find your zeal attractive and contagious.

DELIVERY affects your perceived credibility. Steady and somewhat fast is seen as intelligent and confident. The audience believes it is learning when speakers use vocal variety which is lively and animated. Careful: loud can easily be perceived as untrustworthy.

President Harry Truman said: *"Sincerity, honesty, and a straight-forward manner are more important than special talent or polish."* Be yourself. Be aware of the factors which can affect credibility and trustworthiness. However, you will triumph when your sincerity, honesty, and straight-forward manner strikes the minds and hearts of your listeners.

Content

**"You will get all you want in life
if you help enough other people
get what they want."**
Zig Ziglar

When you sit down to prepare a speech, teasingly remind yourself: *"If you can't make it good, make it short."* Of course you want it to be good. And short takes longer. It is easy to write long, unedited, and sometimes wandering messages. Who said your messages need to be a certain length? If you want, tighten it rigorously. Who is going to complain? Most listeners will be delighted. So, partly humor and partly truth, if you can't make it good, make it short.

Every public speaking class ever taught began with this axiom:
Tell them what you're going to say.
Say it.
Then tell them what you said.
Do not keep the point of your message a secret. Do not presume your audience will get it. Make it clear: Tell the audience what is your point. Then summarize at the end to reinforce learning and the retention of your message.

The beginning

GRAB THE AUDIENCE. Ask yourself *"What is my Attention Getting Device?"* How will I connect with them and compel them to listen for more?

AROUSE CURIOSITY. Start with a question that relates to their interests. For example, *"How would you feel...?"*

TELL A STORY. When listeners hear *"Let me tell you a story..."* they lean forward to listen with interest.

BEGIN WITH A MEMORABLE QUOTATION. Shorter is better. Use a quote that inspires them to think or to nod in agreement.

HUMOR is a great lead, if it works. If it flops, you risk losing their attention.

BEGIN WITH A SINGLE INCIDENT. Mimic news magazines and newspapers. Tell about one person's experience and then apply it to more general applications.

STARTLE with a simple statistic.

USE PERSONAL ILLUSTRATIONS. Pepper your speeches with personal illustrations that could only come from you and no one else. Personal illustrations help you to connect with your people. *"She is one of us"* is the intent. They will know you better as an individual and appreciate that you too have weaknesses, faults, mistakes, or funny things that happen to you. Avoid narcissism and use personal illustrations from the lives of others too, without intruding on their privacy. A readership survey of newspapers found that one of the best-read parts of the paper is the obituaries. People like to read about or hear about other people.

REVEAL YOUR TOPIC. Do not wait too long to make clear your point. Tell them what you are going to talk about.

ACKNOWLEDGE OTHER POINTS OF VIEW. Sincerely accommodate other views, name them, and give them legitimacy.

CONSIDER NUMBERING YOUR POINTS. If you have three points, say so (*"Three strategies for how to become…"*). Examine popular magazines and notice how many articles offer numbered points or bullets such as five tips, six myths, seven strategies, four secrets, three mysteries, eight top methods, ten commandments, and so on.

KEEP YOUR INTRODUCTION BRIEF, usually no more than ten to twenty percent of the message.

AFTER YOU DRAFT YOUR MESSAGE, return to the beginning to re-edit and tie it together with the conclusion.

THE AUDIENCE IS WATCHING YOU from the moment you stand up to speak. Be careful not to spend the first few moments arranging papers, water glass, watch, or fumbling around. Rather, start by making eye contact with every person, take a deep breath, smile, and begin with confidence and control. Put them at ease. Grab attention. A good start will help the whole message go well because *"You got them."*

The ending

It is hard work to end and to find a great conclusion, especially one that lingers in the audience's mind. Often a better ending is already in the body of the speech, a few paragraphs up. When we do not really know how to end, there can be a tendency to keep on talking when an earlier ending would have been preferred. A common criticism of speeches is that they contained multiple conclusions and did not seem like they were ever going to end.

LET THE AUDIENCE KNOW YOU ARE ENDING THE TALK. Near the ending, slow down. Use more pauses. Use briefer sentences. Change your stance, posture, pitch, gestures, tone, or rhythm. Give clues that you are ending: in conclusion, to summarize, let me end by saying…

SUMMARIZE YOUR KEY POINTS to reinforce their understanding – tell them what you said.

CONCLUDE WITH A BANG, not a whimper. End with a quote, a dramatic statement, a story, or refer to the introduction.

TELL WHAT ACTION YOU WISH THEM TO TAKE. This is a persuasive speech. What do you want them to do, think, feel or choose? Make it clear and simple. If this was a sales call, the speech's conclusion closes the deal and asks for the order.

NEVER TELL THEM they are bored or tired. This is a frequent mistake made by after-lunch speakers who tell the audience *"I know you've just eaten and would prefer to take a nap…"* If the meeting is running late, do not call attention to it. Assume people want to hear what you have to say. If you assume they are impatient because you are starting late, they will feel your anxiety.

PRACTICE THE CONCLUSION so that you know it well and can maintain eye contact, control of voice, and management of the ending with a bit of firmness or drama. Slow it down. Use pause and timing for impact. Practice the introduction and the conclusion most of all, because those are the parts that stick in the minds of listeners. That is a fact about lists: people remember the first and last more than the content in the middle. Same with speeches: they will remember and appreciate your opening and closing. Take a deep breath. After you have concluded, smile and make eye contact one last time before turning to sit down.

IT NEVER HURTS to say *"Thank you"* as your last words.

Organizing the body of the speech

Research of public speaking finds that people who heard a well-organized speech believed the speaker to be more competent and trustworthy than did those who heard the scrambled speech – a great plus especially for persuasive speeches. Listeners will notice and appreciate if you are well-organized.

Organize first, write second. Consider the usual order for creating a message: idea, topic, purpose, point, research, organize, write, re-write and edit, practice, practice, practice. Numbering main points helps the audience follow your progression of thought.

In public speaking, every rule is broken, often creatively, but first master the rules. Like abstract artists or jazz musicians, you can break the rules once you know what they are and why you wish to break them.

Following is a typical OUTLINE FORM:
Introduction.
Purpose statement.
Main point. Sub-points never stand alone. Always have at least two sub-points. Avoid too many levels of sub-points.
Second Main point. First sub-point. Second sub-point.
Third Main point. Sub-points. The most important points in any list should be the first and the last.
Conclusion – tell them what you want them to do.

Delivery

> **"Thaw with her gentle persuasion**
> **is more powerful than Thor with his hammer.**
> **The one melts,**
> **the other breaks into pieces."**
> Henry David Thoreau

CONTENT and DELIVERY are the two parts to a speech. They are interwoven. One is not more important than the other, but neglect of one can ruin a presentation. Have you not witnessed speakers who invested almost all on the content? *"He was a nice man,"* they said politely, *"but not very inspiring."* Or consider the opposite: all sizzle, no steak. A speaker can coast on charisma for only so long. Balance your energy on both content and delivery.

The voice of the speaker

Your voice is your tool. A pianist has a piano, a carpenter has a hammer, and the speaker has the voice. Dissect the tool to examine its components:

INTENSITY is the volume of the message. Loud is used for emphasis. When overused, it reduces credibility and turns people off. Did you ever hear a message that was all loud? It makes you wonder *"Why is that person shouting?"* The audience stops paying attention. Soft is used to indicate an intimate connection or confidential information. People lean in forward to listen attentively. All soft loses its effect. To control your voice and appeal to listeners, vary the intensity.

PITCH is how high or low the tone sounds. Changes in pitch gives the voice luster, warmth, and vitality. The opposite is a monotone.

RATE is the speed. Speaking faster creates a sense of action. Speaking slower builds suspense. A speaker who speaks too fast all the time loses the listener. So does the speaker who speaks too slow all the time. The average speaker speaks 125 to 150 words per minute. Daniel Webster spoke at about 90 words per minute. Franklin Roosevelt, 110. John Kennedy, 180. Martin Luther King started his *"I Have a Dream"* speech at 92 words per minute and finished at 145. Fast creates feelings of excitement, happiness, fear, anger, and surprise. Slow is used for sadness or disgust, complex information, intimacy, or to signal a transition or an ending. Do the math: if your speech is 2,000 words long and you speak at about 130 words per minute, you will need fifteen-and-a-half minutes. 3,000 words will require more than twenty-three minutes. Measuring your rate is an impetus to encourage tight writing and vigorous editing.

PAUSE and SILENCE. The Late Mike Wallace from the *Sixty Minutes* TV news program was a master at controlled use of silence. He asked a question, the interviewee answered, and Mike would not respond but reacted with silence, perhaps with a slight hand or facial gesture indicating more was desired. Then… the interviewee continued and that is often when the best parts were revealed. Be intentional about pause when speaking. Use pause to give listeners a breather and also as an emphasis. Make a powerful point and then, with the utmost of comfort, allow it to hang in the air for a moment. To listeners, pauses are brief. The same pause to a speaker can feel like an eternity until you demonstrate that you are comfortable and intentional with the silence.

Mark Twain said: *"The right word may be effective, but no word was ever as effective as a rightly timed pause."*

TIMING. Look at comedians: pauses are critical to a joke or a story. Timing is a skill and an art form, which comes from practice, experience, and attention to delivery. Allow extra time between points, paragraphs, or after an emphasis. Timing is most important with the introduction and the conclusion.

ENUNCIATION is the clarity of the speaker's diction. It is well-pronounced rather than slurred. Many listeners delight in listening to a speaker with clear enunciation.

VOCAL VARIETY is to combine all the components of a speaker's voice in order to master the use of the tool for the pleasure of the listener. Variety of intensity, pitch, and rate provide interest and add spice to the delivery of the content.

WHEN USING A MICROPHONE, be natural. The mic is your friend. Kiss the mic. Let it be close to your lips. Use the mic to manage control and variety. A good sound system allows the speaker to talk with his or her people rather than to bellow at them. If you were speaking to a group too large but without a mic, you might find that all you could do was shout, which is a most uncomfortable arrangement. If possible, practice with your sound system so that you can manage its advantages to your benefit.

DO NOT BE DISCOURAGED BY WHAT YOU CANNOT DO WELL. Some of the most famous speakers in history and today have had challenges when it came to speaking. Abraham Lincoln possessed a harsh and penetrating voice. Winston Churchill suffered from a lisp and a stammer. Bruce Willis, Julia Roberts, and James Earl Jones were stutterers.

And then, there was Moses who replied to God: *"I have never been a good speaker. I wasn't one before you spoke to me, and I'm not one now. I am slow at speaking, and I can never think of what to say."* (Exodus 4:10, Contemporary English Version). The key is not that a speaker suffers from a speaking challenge but that he or she overcomes it and learns to control the voice. As Helen Keller observed *"Although the world is full of suffering, it is also full of the overcoming of it."* Lean into your strengths and do not be distracted by what you cannot do well. You have overcome challenges in your life before and you can overcome challenges when you give a speech.

The body of the speaker

Actions speak louder than words, especially in public speaking where non-verbal communication can amplify a speaker's message or contradict it. You communicate subtle messages by your posture, gestures, eyes and facial expressions – sometimes without knowing it, often not intended, and frequently misinterpreted by the audience. Heighten your awareness of the power of the non-verbal. Herodotus, the Greek historian, grasped this truth: *"People trust their ears less than their eyes."*

Consider the elements of non-verbal communication:

POSTURE: When you are in a conversation and lean forward, you appear to be listening attentively. If you were to slouch back, hands behind the neck and staring at the ceiling, the other might assume you are not paying attention. How you stand behind the podium signals listeners that you care… or do not care… about your topic. Leaning forward indicates increased intensity, especially if coupled with a softer tone. Shifting your stance indicates a transition.

If intended, it helps listeners know you are shifting your points. If not intended, it distracts and can cause attention to run off the rails, which can take a few minutes to get back on. If you mindlessly stare out the window, up at the ceiling, or off into middle distance, you come across as not paying attention to your speaking. Leaning on the lectern suggests a relaxed and informal moment. Doing it non-stop suggests you are taking your message lightly. Standing too rigid, perhaps because of nervousness, can indicate a rigidity of views. Practice your message before a mirror to help gauge the effectiveness of posture on your delivery.

GESTURES. Gestures aid in getting the point across if used effectively. Otherwise, they appear amateurish. It is okay to talk with your hands if it is not too distracting. You want listeners to listen to you more than to watch you. Gestures are more likely to distract than enable, which is why their use should be practiced and skillfully employed. Gestures should not draw attention to themselves or distract from your message, but should appear natural and spontaneous (even though they are practiced).

DISTANCE. In conversation, how far away should you stand when speaking to another person? Answer: about an arm's length. Any closer leads to discomfort by the other. Further away, and you seem distant. Removed. Likewise when speaking. What if you are high up on stage and your audience is sitting in the back rows? To you, it feels distant. Perhaps they like it that way. Notice how people talk about the speaker "up" there. Removed. Above them, literally and perhaps in other ways. Not on their level. Anything you can do to remove the distance and speak on their level will serve you well. If possible, come down to floor level... eye level... with your audience. If they sit in the rear and won't come forward, pick up the podium and move it closer to them. Or, if you can, scratch the podium and walk to stand closer to them.

EYE CONTACT. Your listeners want to be seen. They want to know that you, the speaker, see them, connect with them, and speak with them rather than at them. Maintain eye contact for about three-quarters of the time you are speaking. Less than that and you are likely reading your manuscript which is about the worst delivery a speaker can make. Let your gaze linger upon each person for a few seconds rather than for a fleeting moment. When you catch yourself quickly gazing up from your notes, looking at no one in particular, and staring into middle distance, then you know you have some work to do on your delivery style. You want your listeners to feel seen.

MANNERISMS. One speaker jiggled the keys and change in his pocket for the entirety of his speech. That is what the audience watched. Another unconsciously groomed her hair and plucked lint from her jacket. Another toyed with his ear, as though to pluck wax out of it and then look at his finger. Yuk. Mannerisms can undo all the labor you invest in creating your speech.

PERSONAL APPEARANCE. Listeners see you before they hear you. They begin to form impressions about you before you even open your mouth. How is the audience dressed? Should you dress the same or more formally? It is usually best to err in favor of over-dressing than under-dressing. Your presentation is not a rehearsal. It is the real deal. Get a haircut, a good night's sleep, eat a good meal, bring some Rolaids, and polish your shoes. How you look and take care of yourself counts to the audience. Dress the part. What would you look like at your professional best? Dress like you take your opportunity to speak seriously and as an honor. However, if you feel phony dressing up for public speaking, that too will come across as a distraction. Whether or not we like being judged by our appearance, it is a fact that personal appearance is a part of the delivery.

Notice politicians, how the jackets come off, the ties are loosened, the top button is unbuttoned and the shirtsleeves are rolled up. Does it seem phony? *"He is one of us,"* is the thought about making formal attire seem informal. Casual. Relaxed. In Control. Practice reading the appearance of your audience to suggest how your attire might communicate a message.

THEY ARE WATCHING YOU. Speakers can err in thinking they are watched from their opening line to their closing word. Not so. The audience is watching you from the moment you enter. They watch what you are doing with your notes, with your hands, with your water, with others on the podium, and with your eyes and posture. They watch how you rise to speak, how you approach the podium, appearing calm, poised and confident… despite how you really feel. They notice if you immediately rush to get down to business or if you take a few moments to build rapport and acknowledge them. They appreciate when you take it easy at first, take a deep breath, smile and then begin. Your audience is like a phone which cannot be hung up. After you conclude, they are still watching you. They watch how you turn, how you smile, how you sit, and how you compose yourself after a presentation that utilized every nerve and muscle in your body to the point of sheer exhaustion… and yet still look refreshed and in control. Do not get paranoid about it, but neither neglect the reality that everything you do is a part of the message and has the potential to communicate.

Use visual aids

An average speaker who uses visual aids will come across as better prepared, more credible, and more professional than a dynamic speaker who does not use visual aids. Public speaking research indicates that visual aids can increase the persuasiveness of a speech by more than 40%. Poorly done, it undermines your best efforts. When well-prepared and executed, it amplifies your presentation, your audience remembers it best and appreciates it more.

When I taught public speaking at a university, I emphasized two points: 1) Use visual aids at your own risk. If they fail, so do you. 2) It is usually well worth the risk and you get extra points for making it work.

PLUSSES OF VISUAL AIDS. Visual aids enhance the clarity of a presentation and make vivid your points. They add interest as well as another dimension for the audience to watch. Visual aids are also known to help combat stage fright because they shift attention away from the speaker to the object being shown. Visual aids are best regarded because they aid in retention. People will remember your object lesson. It stays with them. Making a presentation where you present pro and con arguments? Consider using two podiums or a white hat and a black hat so the audience will easily recognize the side you are taking.

MINUSES OF VISUAL AIDS. If not done well, objects can distract rather than reinforce the speaker's message. It can appear gimmicky, even childish. Generally, the plusses outweigh the minuses. What can you lose? You have much to gain.

USING CHARTS AND GRAPHS. If you do it, keep it extraordinarily simple. If they can't see it or understand it, you lose.

USING VIDEO, with a TV recorder or a computer: a sloppy presentation is far worse than no visual aid. The audience wants to see you as a speaker, not as an equipment operator. *"This doesn't seem to be working today"* is never acceptable. If you have not prepared to do it well and double-checked every possible glitch, do not use it.

MAKE SURE YOUR AID IS LARGE ENOUGH. Holding up a small object which can only be seen by those in the first or second row will sink your ship. Words projected on a screen which cannot be seen viewed by those in the back row are wasted. Make it LARGE.

AVOID HAVING YOUR BACK TO THE AUDIENCE. Always face them, not away from them. When using a blackboard, easel pad, or PowerPoint, if you are not facing your audience you are facing the wrong way.

DISPLAY THE AIDS ONLY WHILE TALKING ABOUT THEM. Do not leave the screen on after you have moved on to the next point.

TALK TO YOUR AUDIENCE, NOT TO YOUR VISUAL AID. The aid is just that: an aid to help you make your point. Be obsessed with your audience, not your objects.

USE POWERPOINT AT YOUR OWN RISK. When done well, it can dazzle. Usually, it is not done well. *"This was working when I practiced, but something is not working right now."* You lose. Or, the speaker forgot to pre-arrange with someone to turn out the lights or close the shades. You lose. Or, instead of a screen, the blank wall does not display the images well.

Or, the audience sits and studies your entire desktop while you fumble to get it working, focusing all your attention on a keyboard and mouse instead of on your people. That results, of course, in no eye contact. Use of PowerPoint: high risk, high gain. If you cannot master it, do not use it.

Using statistics

Make statistics and numbers come alive to your listeners. Use techniques to help them grasp the broader concept.

LESS IS MORE. Too many statistics are a killer. Use sparingly.

BETTER TO UNDERSTATE. Do not acquire a reputation for exaggeration. When you understate, listeners will round up themselves.

USE *"GREATER THAN"* RATHER THAN *"ALMOST."* It is a more powerful case to say that *"More than 60% of Americans are planning to purchase a new car"* rather than *"Almost 70 percent of Americans are planning to purchase a new car." "More than"* supersedes *"almost."*

MAKE STATISTICS CREDIBLE and DIRECTLY RELATED to your point. Did you know that 57% of people in an automobile accident last year had eaten a pickle in the previous month? True, but not related or credible.

USE RELIABLE SOURCES. Would you trust tobacco companies to give you credible statistics on teen smoking? How about the AMA? The NRA? Lobbying groups contain obvious biases. Quote reliable sources to bolster your position.

THE AUDIENCE WILL NOT REMEMBER THE NUMBERS, BUT THE IMPACT LASTS. It is not important that they grasp or memorize the statistics you quote. Rather, make an impact with them.

DEFINE YOUR TERMS. "*Average*" can apply to a mean, median, or mode. Help your listeners understand what you mean by average. The median household income in an affluent town is $125,000 a year. The mean household income in the same town is $85,000. When quoting averages of such disparity, define your terms.

MAKE IT PERSONAL. For example, if talking about the divorce rate, count off by twos and ask every number two to stand. Half the audience is standing. That is how many marriages fail. Personalization drives home the point.

ROUND OFF. 71.976% means nothing and is instantly forgotten. Seven out of ten is remembered. It is not necessary to say *"about seven out of ten."* The broad rounded-off estimate is sufficient and well understood.

DOCUMENT YOUR STATISTICS. Where did you get them? The "*internet*" is not a credible source. Quote original sources wherever possible, even if obtained via the internet.

SIMPLICITY RULES. When using statistics, there are three key points: simplicity, simplicity, and simplicity. Keep it simple, understandable, and easily remembered.

WHER POSSIBLE, FAVOR STORIES to statistics. Being with a story and work out from there. To begin with statistics is deadly. Instead, tell a story, and listeners will lean forward to receive your words.

Use inclusive language and recognized the multicultural composition of your audience

Use words that illustrate that you are sensitive to your audience's composition.

AVOID THE USE OF "*MAN*" when referring to both men and women. It is easy and inclusive to say *humankind* instead of *mankind*. While some may not care, most will be grateful for your sensitivity. Do not make all illustrations of one gender, but vary them.

AVOID STEREOTYPING jobs and social roles by gender. If illustrations about senior executives are male and illustrations about support staff are female, that indicates a speaker out of touch with reality.

AVOID IDENTIFYING PERSONAL TRAITS THAT ARE UNRELATED TO THE TOPIC. A shooter on a college campus was headlined as a South Korean. Why was that important to name? He was also a male, a twenty year old, a southerner, a college sophomore, a computer major, left handed, a member of the National Rifle Association, and bi-polar. Headlining his country of origin diminished regard for South Koreans.

PREFER NAMES THAT GROUPS USE TO IDENTIFY THEMSELVES. This changes constantly, but should you use black or African American or Negro or people of color? Should you say lesbian or gay or homosexual? Chinese Americans, Asian or Oriental? Native Americans, Indians, or first Americans? Use sensitivity in selecting descriptions of groups and choose terms that they prefer.

Rest to be at your best.

Scientists have discovered that the best preparation for public speaking is sleep. Sleep is better than cramming or over preparing. Get a good night's sleep. Take a nap beforehand. Feel rested, ready, and in control. Take no risk to become exhausted. A tired speaker will create a tired audience. Plan your schedule so that you feel rested, relaxed, ready and prepared. Those who prepare at last minute will be found out by your audience, who will not appreciate a lack of preparation, research, thought and practice.

Use your weakness

In college, I became a tutor for students in a public speaking course. This experience inspired me to teach public speaking at a university later in life. The professor assigned me to tutor a young woman with multiple sclerosis. *"This girl is going to fail,"* said the professor. There was no way she could stand before a class and give a speech. She drooled. She had uncontrollable spasms. She could not keep her balance standing up. She was sort of a hunchback. She stuttered. She was scared to death, spoke in a monotone, and was very easily distracted.

People did not like being around her... their eyes avoided looking at her. After meeting with her, I did not see any way possible and was about to give up and resign the assignment. Then the inspiration struck about to make this work: USE YOUR WEAKNESS. Who in the world could give a better talk on what it feels like to live with MS than this young woman?

She and I worked hours a day on her ten-minute speech. She would tell about MS. She was easily distracted. So, I would sit and listen to her speech and knock a pile of textbooks on the floor. I would yawn loudly. Once I even burped. I would stand up and go look out the window. I did everything I could to distract her, so by the time she gave her speech, she was made of steel.

In practice, she read her speech in a monotone. I went up, grabbed it from the podium, ripped it in half and told her *Tell your own story. Don't tell about MS. Tell about what it feels like to have it. Use your weakness. Tell about what you know.*

In practice, she still looked down at the podium. I removed the podium and the table. She had to stand there with nothing between her and the audience. I would walk around the room and tell her: *Look me in the eyes the whole time you are speaking.* She must have practiced that ten-minute speech for twenty hours.

The day came for her speech. She arrived just as the class was starting. Her normally frizzly hair was all made-up by her friends in the dorm. She wore a professional looking black dress, a string of pearls. She was radiant. She felt good about herself. She was ready.

When it was time, she walked to the front of the class, took a breath, stood up straight, looked every student deep into the eyes, smiled, and told her own story of what it feels like to have MS. With poise and confidence, she poked fun at her spastic episodes and some of the nervous reactions she received. She explained the rejection, the looks she caught out of the corner of her eye, what it felt like to live in chronic pain and to always be fatigued.

They laughed, they cried, they relaxed, and they learned. As she spoke, you could hear a pin drop, so riveted were they on her every word. Ten minutes later, she finished. There was total silence. Tears welled up in the eyes of her classmates and rolled down the cheeks of the professor.

And then, as though by silent signal, the entire class rose to their feet and applauded her with a standing ovation that lasted half as long as her speech..

Use your weakness and tell about what you know or feel.

Visualize yourself succeeding.

So much of public speaking is attitude: Believe in yourself. Believe that you can succeed. Take inspiration from the Roman poet Virgil: *"He can conquer who believes he can."* She can conquer who believes she can. A corporate CEO nailed it: *"If you think you can or can't, you are right."*

Booker T. Washington said *"Success is to be measured not so much by the position that one has reached in life as by the obstacles which he has overcome while trying to succeed."*

George Bernard Shaw wrote *"Some people see things as they are and ask 'Why?' Others dream things that could be and ask 'Why not?'"* Why not you?

Management expert Stephen Covey (*Seven Habits of Highly Effective People*) says: *"You can visualize in every area of your life. Before a performance, a sales presentation, a difficult confrontation, or the daily challenge of meeting a goal, see it clearly, vividly, relentlessly, and over and over again. Create an internal 'comfort zone.' Then, when you get into the situation, it isn't foreign. It doesn't scare you."*

He tells about Dr. Charles Garfield, with one doctorate in mathematics and another in psychology, is a researcher in the study of peak performers. He researched peak performers in athletics, in business, and with NASA, watching the astronauts rehearse everything on earth, again and again, in a simulated environment before they went to space. One of the main findings of his research showed that peak performers are visualizers. They see it. They visualize it. They experience it before they actually do it. They begin with the end in mind.

A trapeze artist instructed his students on how to perform on the high trapeze bar. After teaching about what to do, he told them *"Now, get up there and demonstrate your ability."* One student looked up at that insecure perch and he froze. Struck with fear, he had a vision of falling to the ground. His fright was so deep, he could not move a muscle. *"I can't do it!"* He said. The instructor put his arm around the boy's shoulder and said, *"Son, you can do it, and I will tell you how."* Then he shared his trade secret. He said, *"Throw your heart over the bar and your body will follow."*

Visualize it. Picture yourself succeeding. Imagine yourself speaking effectively, clearly, and well as you connect with your audience. Dream it, because, as an Olympic gold medalist observed *"If you can't dream it, you can't do it."* Visualized yourself succeeding as an effective and persuasive public speaker and you will throw your heart over the bar.

# # #

About the Author

John Zehring served in executive leadership of higher education and as senior pastor to United Church of Christ congregations in New England. He taught college courses in public speaking, psychology, creative writing, and administration and authored more than forty books and eBooks. John is listed in Marquis' <u>Who's Who in America</u> and is a recipient of their Albert Nelson Marquis Lifetime Achievement Award.

Public Speaking Books by John Zehring

Persuade them: Public Speaking to Convince

Public Speaking for Executives, Leaders & Managers

Eulogies, Introductions and Special Occasion Speeches:
Tips for When You Are Asked to Speak Well of Another

Clergy Guide to Sermon Preparation

Clergy Public Speaking Guide:
Improve What You Already Do Well

www.ingramcontent.com/pod-product-compliance
Lightning Source LLC
Chambersburg PA
CBHW070824220526
45466CB00002B/754